T0391604

HELPING OUT OTHERS

I HELP OUT MY RELATIVES

AMY CULLIFORD

A Crabtree Roots Book

Crabtree Publishing
crabtreebooks.com

School-to-Home Support for Caregivers and Teachers

This book helps children grow by letting them practice reading. Here are a few guiding questions to help the reader with building his or her comprehension skills. Possible answers appear here in red.

Before Reading:

• What do I think this book is about?
  • *I think this book is about helping relatives.*
  • *I think this book is about the types of jobs I can do to help my relatives.*

• What do I want to learn about this topic?
  • *I want to learn what jobs I could do to make my relatives happy.*
  • *I want to learn why it is important to help relatives.*

During Reading:

• I wonder why...
  • *I wonder why it feels nice to help my relatives.*
  • *I wonder why there are so many different jobs to do around the house.*

• What have I learned so far?
  • *I have learned that it's fun to help Grandma make cookies.*
  • *I have learned that my relatives appreciate when I help them.*

After Reading:

• What details did I learn about this topic?
  • *I have learned that visiting my relatives is important.*
  • *I have learned that helping relatives is fun.*

• Read the book again and look for the vocabulary words.
  • *I see the word **relatives** on page 3 and the word **groceries** on page 5. The other vocabulary words are found on page 14.*

I want to help out
my **relatives**.

I help my aunt put away the **groceries**.

I help with **recycling**.

I help Grandma make **cookies**.

I help my uncle with the **dishes**.

I like to help out
my relatives!

Word List
Sight Words

away	make	the
help	my	to
I	out	want
like	put	with

Words to Know

cookies **dishes** **groceries**

recycling **relatives**

38 Words

I want to help out my **relatives**.

I help my aunt put away the **groceries**.

I help with **recycling**.

I help Grandma make **cookies**.

I help my uncle with the **dishes**.

I like to help out my relatives!

I HELP OUT MY RELATIVES

Written by: Amy Culliford

Designed by: Rhea Wallace

Series Development: James Earley

Proofreader: Melissa Boyce

Educational Consultant: Marie Lemke M.Ed.

Photographs:
Shutterstock: Chomplearn: cover; Pixel-shot: p. 1, 10;
    PeopleImages: p. 3, 4; Maples Images: p. 6; Lorn: p. 9;
    Irnya Images: p. 12

Crabtree Publishing

crabtreebooks.com   800-387-7650
Copyright © 2025 Crabtree Publishing
All rights reserved. No part of this
publication may be reproduced, stored
in a retrieval system or be transmitted
in any form or by any means, electronic,
mechanical, photocopying, recording,
or otherwise, without the prior written
permission of Crabtree Publishing. In
Canada: We acknowledge the financial
support of the Government of Canada
through the Canada Book Fund for our
publishing activities.

Printed in the USA
062024/CG20240201

Published in Canada
Crabtree Publishing
616 Welland Ave.
St. Catharines, Ontario
L2M 5V6

Published in the United States
Crabtree Publishing
347 Fifth Ave
Suite 1402-145
New York, NY 10016

Library and Archives Canada Cataloguing in Publication
Available at Library and Archives Canada

Library of Congress Cataloging-in-Publication Data
Available at the Library of Congress

Hardcover: 978-1-0398-3828-4
Paperback: 978-1-0398-3913-7
Ebook (pdf): 978-1-0398-3997-7
Epub: 978-1-0398-4069-0